Hidden Valley Dispatches

after Cold Mountain, Stonehouse,
and the Chinese master poets

with gratitude to Red Pine
for his incomparable translations

poems
Al Zolynas

art
Mary Kowit

Gorilla Press
established 4004 B.C.E.

Gorilla Press
P.O. Box 184
Potrero, CA 91963-0184

Garden Oak Press
gardenoakpress.com
gardenoakpress@gmail.com

First published by Gorilla Press through Garden Oak Press on September 1, 2025.

ISBN-13: 979-8-9879532-5-9

Printed in the United States of America

For Arlie, my Dearest (1944 - 2024)

1

Standing on the tile of the shower floor
I adjust the nozzle for finer spray
comfort driven suburbanite that I am
the ex-emperor of America is being stripped
lacking a cold stream to lie in
I wash my ears in municipal water
tepid it is but loosens the wax
a distant music drifts in

2

In our household of two persons
one of us has fallen ill
and is now being cared for by the other
who has also been sick betimes
and was nursed by that one
one and other no other than one

3

Here in Hidden Valley
the valley is neither hidden nor much of a valley
if contrast between up and down is any measure
though I suppose when the first Spaniards came
the word *escondido* came to their lips
the Kumeyaay never forgot their name for home
and I've lived here for almost four decades
the place to hang my fedora
as in the other 30 places I've abided in
along the Way

4

Dozey afternoon on recliners in front of sound-muted
  tv
cool summer breeze filters through screen door
post-surgical wound healing we hope
pulse and burble of wound vac drags us down into
  sleep
even through sharp pain for one of us
visit to oncologist in the offing
small plane drones overhead on approach to Palomar
  airport
dearest where to now when nowhere calls anymore?

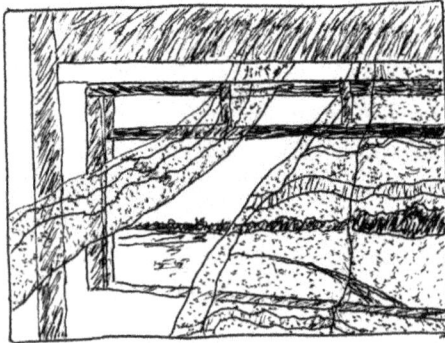

5

To qualify as an "after" poet to Cold Mountain *et al*
I must write a poem about the moon
wish I could claim I sat outside my hut
as the full moon rose above our local peak
but no I just caught it when I came downstairs
to my wife's call in the middle of the night
a strange light she said
was reflected in the wall mirror
and wouldn't let her sleep
as I reached up to lower the shade
there the moon was
full face shining through pine branches
I daresay just as you saw her Hanshan
all those years ago

6

So our little meditation group met on Zoom this
   morning
makeshift cyber-Zen center convened once a week
today 9 on-screen boxes with live head shots
of my fellow practitioners of the Way
I won't say we looked like Hollywood Squares
but if we did why not?
worse things to resemble than all those actors
who showed us how to live and how not
through the sacrifices of their own living
yes they acted parts but always
at the expense of their own lives
and for our life

7

Five five-by-fives

The sub-urban life
so not your mountain
yet we two-leggeds
across centuries
can still lock eyebrows

•

I sit like you sat
mat topped by cushion
under the same moon
mystery of sound
distant coyote

•

I have what I need
even what I want
blessèd in old age
while good health holds out
inner child can sing

•

In the spaceless space
I join you Hanshan
nothing has moved since
gibbons howled for you
coyotes for me

•

Thirty-seven years
in Hidden Valley
it was yesterday
when we moved in here
to bursting fireworks

8

Trying to preserve something of the elemental
in this modern life
not so easy where all is mediated
as through tv through radio through Google
I will now make and enjoy a cup of green tea
mediated through its little porous paper bag

9

Stonehouse cancers must have been available
in your dynasty though the atmosphere
undoubtedly was more robust and protective
not like our own ozone-depleted and thinned-out air
here our epidermi host various blotches
life-threatening or not they must be excised
followed into the body with immunotherapy
or chemo or radiation
you didn't have those did you
just herbs and acupuncture
we still have those
quite popular too

10

Fenggan and Shide here we have a particular bird
the California Northern Mockingbird
whose complex melody of trills chirps chucks
and glissandos never fails to cheer my heart
I hear it throughout the spring and summer
bird perched on growing vertical sprig of highest pine
or on the caret peak of suburban roof
I am here she says and
I can sound just like you

11

Tennis on the silent screen across the room
two fellows vying for the prize
they slide across the clay or skid on the grass
hit smashes and dinks and jaw-dropping passing
shots
to me their score is meaningless
but when I look up from my notebook
I can't help be momentarily drawn in
grace of human form leaping
ball dispatched neatly on the intersecting lines
of a far corner

12

Lunch today was an egg and bean and cheese burrito
I daresay unavailable in your neck of the mountains
lo these many centuries ago
tomorrow we'll eat Thai or Indian or Chinese or
  Japanese
when I have broccoli and rice
how can I not remember you
great mountain forest
bonsai-ed in my Asian Bowl

13

Headless in Hidden Valley
which is to say Hidden Valley
is where my head used to be
now Hidden Valley has fallen
into my head and inside outside
have dropped all meaning

14

Double duty double chores for one
while the other heals
not a situation preferred by either
healer focusses on getting well
accepting pain as sign of healing
double doer focuses on doing the next thing
which remembered is all
there ever is to do

15

Here in Hidden Valley
we too have made concoctions
taken herbs and supplements
followed programs
kept up exercises
all in pursuit of immortality
we've even given up the more obvious attempts
but have remained wedded to subtle strategies
like reminding ourselves of transience
oh we are good at noting impermanence
from the point of view of our own
presumed permanence

16

As we seem to be Cold Mountain's future
(he wrote he wanted to send us a message)
perhaps you somewhere years hence
can be Hidden Valley's future
the dispatch is still the same:
come to Cold Mountain some day or to
Hidden Valley or to that place where you are
right now that is re-turn
with just the slightest backward step
sink down into that no-place of infinite peace

17

Beyond the backyard's paling fence pine trees
beyond them a valley of houses
my neighbors these days
a horizon of waving hills and clouds beyond them
sky all lit by its particular time of day
Hanshan you poor bastard
too bad you can't hear
the nearby freeway traffic the small-engine plane
passing all aglint overhead

18

Meditation outside is always nice
eyes at half mast peripheral vision engaged
or later lids dropped
garden's green a memory
any bird sounds now come without the bird
just that plaintive call
from the heart of things
which only deepens the silence

19

A new café has popped up
not so far by So Cal standards
i.e. 10-minute drive
so sitting here now over ceramic cappuccino cup
lovely leaf pattern swirled into its foam
by expert Italian-accented barista
all around the café Halloween skulls
mini skeletons fake RIP gravestones
unconscious *memento moris*
a few live plants too
among us coffee-sipping mortals

20

And so I must ask
after a lifetime of writing
what does poetry have to do with awakening
at its worst nothing but mawkish self-indulgence
and I've been guilty of that
but at its best perhaps
a celebration of what's now and here
words as pointers and reminders
fascinating signs

21

Wife walking now though with a limp
healing slowly
slower than she would like
than I would too for that matter
apparently some things can't be rushed
summer was full of pain
autumn too but less
with winter icummen in it's a joyful
sing goddamn we're hoping for

22

Four four-by-fours

Immuno three
tomorrow morn
with its fatigue
hope it's working

•

Tibetans say
rigpa is here
right now and now
let's remember

•

Computer chess
problem rated
three thousand plus
gimme a hint

•

Massage feels good
all kinks worked out
temporary
contentment now

23

Dead friends poets artists visit in dreams
propose absurdities that make sense in the dream
   world
one dead poet friend says I must only write poems
nothing else energy for creativity alone
cut all the rest out let it go
drive all ambitions into one
in that subtle realm it resonates
on waking I remember how many other things
besides the business of fracturing iambs
Stephen D would get himself into

24

Hanshan all well and good to lie down
in a mountain stream and rinse your ears out
sit through a long night with nothing
but a sputtering candle and hooting owls for company
you were of your time I of mine
though God knows we've both chased the timeless
often enough in the ways passed on to us
ah another Amazon delivery at my doorstep
out with its merch
another cardboard box
to break down and recycle

25

The big motors race up and down the parkway
waking me and filling my ears with dread
I listen till I no longer hear them
that moment when the faintest sound
crosses the membrane to no-sound
once just before the absence
came a distant crumpling thump
followed soon enough by faint sirens
a Saturday night around 4 am
in our Hidden Valley

26

Text exchange between Fenggan and Hanshan
yo you in your cave this morning?
where else dude?
wait there I'm bringing fresh radishes from the
  monastery
no moonshine?
no but I read yr new poem on the flat rock by the
  stream
    the one about the girls with skirts embroidered
    with butterflies of gold cool man
ah yes that one cost me a night's sleep
    hurry with the radishes I can already taste them

27

Fellas you weren't into golf back then were you?
it's kinda what nature's come to hereabouts
I haven't chased the little white sphere in years now
not since my playing partners moved on
still it was nice walking the green fairways under
the California live oaks wrapped in warm spring air
the occasional swing perfect in its arc
so perfect you knew it had been waiting
since before the Big Bang

28

Three three-by-threes and one one-by-one

traffic now
moving slow
breathe and wait

•

No haiku
short poem
nonetheless

•

Lunch at noon
gym at three
nap at five

•

As
Is

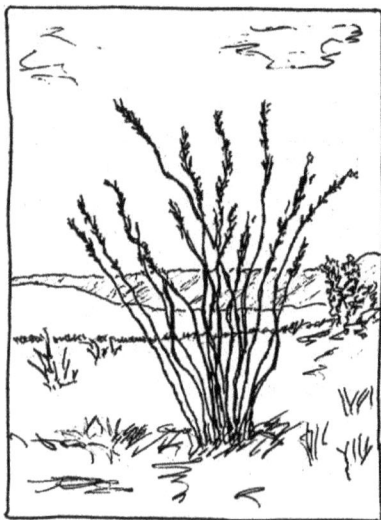

Al Zolynas is the author of ***The New Physics, Under Ideal Conditions, The Same Air, Near and Far,*** and **A World Once Known**. He has co-edited two poetry anthologies: *Men of Our Time* and *The Poetry of Men's Lives: An International Anthology.* He teaches Zen meditation in Escondido, California.

Hidden Valley Dispatches is a short celebration of the influences of old Chinese poetry on the poet. Through the incomparable translations of Red Pine (Bill Porter), Zolynas explores his timeless connection to poets like Hanshan and Stonehouse through the particulars of his own life in "Hidden Valley."

The poet's wife Arlie was diagnosed with melanoma in the spring of 2023. The poems here were written during her slow recovery from surgery during that summer and fall.

Mary Kowit retired after working in information technology for nearly 20 years. Married for 47 years to the poet Steve Kowit, she has been a vegetarian all her adult life and is an avid advocate for animal rights. She now lives in the backcountry of East San Diego County.

www.ingramcontent.com/pod-product-compliance
Lightning Source LLC
Chambersburg PA
CBHW070351070426
42446CB00050BA/3210